Safe Memory Management in Rust
Concurrency without Data Races

Table of Contents

Chapter 1. Introduction

Delving into the elegantly complex crux of modern computing, this Special Report proudly presents "Safe Memory Management in Rust: Concurrency without Data Races". Anticipate a lucid, step-by-step journey through the revolutionary principles embedded deep within Rust, a language renowned for its unique take on memory management and concurrency. Our report demystically unravels Rust's approach to ensuring concurrent computing free of the notorious data races, balancing accurate technical insights and digestible explanations. Whether you're a seasoned developer or a curious beginner, this exploration of Rust's unique paradigm will become a cornerstone in your understanding of safer, more efficient multi-threaded programming.

Chapter 2. Understanding the Rust Programming Language

Rust programming language, by design, spearheads the modern computing era with a unique approach towards safe memory management and concurrency. It offers a different perspective on these traditional concepts, enabling developers to build robust, concurrent programs that evade notorious programming challenges, such as data races.

===Basics of Rust

Rust is a system programming language that aims to provide memory safety, concurrency, and performance with a focus on zero cost abstractions, minimal runtime, and improved productivity. Mozilla Research birthed the project in 2010, seeking to create a safe yet practical language.

The core uniqueness of Rust lies in its powerful abstractions, enabling high-level programming constructs without compromising on lower-level control. Its primary goals of zero cost abstractions, memory safety, concurrency, and minimal runtime make it an attractive choice for developers.

===Memory Management in Rust

Memory management has been a complex challenge in programming. While languages like Java, Python, and JavaScript automate memory management through Garbage Collection (GC), this can lead to unpredictable performance glitches. On the other hand, languages like C and C++ allow manual memory management, resulting in potential errors and security vulnerabilities. Rust's approach to this is an intelligent middle ground, advocating a compile-time ownership system with zero cost abstraction.

The backbone of Rust's memory management is its system of ownership with a set of rules that the compiler checks at compile time. No garbage collector is needed. You have maximum control over the hardware, like in C++, but you have the compiler helping you to rigorously ensure safety.

In Rust, all memory allocations, whether on the heap or the stack, have an owner. When the owner goes out of scope, Rust automatically deallocates the memory. This mechanic, combined with Rust's focus on references and borrowing, lays the foundation for understanding its unique approach towards safe concurrency.

===Understanding Ownership, Borrowing, and Lifetimes

Rust provides three key features related to memory safety and concurrency: Ownership, Borrowing, and Lifetimes.

- `Ownership` in Rust defines the scope of application data, specifying that every value in Rust has a unique owner, and once the owner goes out of scope, the value will be 'dropped', and the memory it holds is freed.

- `Borrowing` is Rust's way of allowing access to data without taking ownership. It differentiates between mutable and immutable borrows, ensuring at compile-time that either you can have multiple immutable references or a single mutable one.

- `Lifetimes` play an essential role in describing the scope for which a reference is valid.

2.1. Concurrency in Rust

Rust's take on concurrency provides the tools to build reliable and efficient concurrent programs in a high-level language design without the risk of data races. It employs the concepts of ownership, borrowing, and lifetimes to ensure safe concurrency practices.

Rust's channel() function further strengthens its concurrent processing functionality, facilitating data sharing between threads. This function creates a multi-producer, single-consumer channel, implying multiple threads can send data, but a single thread will receive and use the data.

Rust's concurrency model also supports the `spawn` function, enabling straightforward thread creation. Rust uses the ownership model and typing system thoroughly, ensuring that data races are caught during compilation.

===Error Handling in Rust

Error handling is an integral part of any programming language. Rust promotes returning an `enum` type Result, which can be `Ok` or `Err`, over exceptions used in many other languages. Rust doesn't have exceptions. Instead, it has the type `Result<T, E>` for recoverable errors and `panic!` macro that stops execution when the program encounters an unrecoverable error.

===The Future of Rust

Over the past few years, Rust has gained increasing popularity among developers, as evidenced by the Stack Overflow Developer Survey, where it has been voted the most loved programming language five years in a row. Its focus on performance, memory safety, concurrency, and most importantly, developer experience, makes it a compelling tool for future software development.

Rust is already being adopted by some of the most significant tech giants like Microsoft, Amazon AWS, and Google. As we venture deeper into an era of Internet of Things and edge computing, Rust's ability to operate at a low level, provide zero-cost abstractions, and maintain memory-safety and thread-safety becomes even more critical.

This chapter has delved into the foundational concepts and unique aspects of the Rust programming language. A comprehension of these concepts will form a gateway into Rust's approach to safe concurrency and efficient memory management, which we will explore in detail in the next chapters. This unique approach presents an exciting prospect in the world of software development, promising more safe and resilient systems than ever before.

Chapter 3. Primer on Memory Management

Understanding memory management requires a grasp of essential concepts and terminologies. This section will elucidate the prime facets of memory management and elaborate on the role and implementation of memory management in widespread programming languages, setting the perfect stage for understanding memory management in Rust.

3.1. What is Memory Management?

Memory management refers to the process of controlling, coordinating, and managing computer memory. It involves keeping track of each byte in a system's memory and determining which parts are in use and which ones can be repurposed. Effective memory management is critical for the optimal performance of a system as it ensures efficient use of the memory.

In the context of programming, memory management is majorly about allocation and deallocation of memory to programs. This can either be managed automatically (by the runtime system) or manually, by the programmer.

3.2. Manual Memory Management

In manual memory management, programmers have direct control over which variables occupy the system's memory and when they should be removed. Languages like C and C++ follow this paradigm. Here, the programmer uses specific language constructs to allocate memory (`malloc` or `new`) and deallocate memory (`free` or `delete`).

```
int *my_pointer = (int*) malloc(sizeof(int) * 5); //
Allocate memory
free(my_pointer); // Free memory
```

The advantage of manual memory management is the precise control over the system's memory. However, this approach comes with considerable responsibility and potential for mistakes—leaving memory blocks unreleased (memory leaks) or trying to access memory spaces that have been already freed (dangling pointers).

3.3. Automatic Memory Management

Automatic memory management alleviates the burden of manual memory management by automatically managing the memory resources. This management is typically accomplished using a garbage collector (GC). High-level languages like Python, Java, and C# follow this approach.

In automatic memory management, programmers do not need to deallocate memory explicitly. The garbage collector tracks all allocated memory, and when it determines that some part of the memory is unreachable or no longer in use, it reclaims it.

The major upside of automatic memory management is the reduced chances of memory leaks or dangling pointers. But this convenience can translate into overhead for the garbage collector, leading to performance sags during garbage collection.

3.4. Understanding the Stack and Heap

Memory for your program's variables can exist in two places: the stack and the heap. Both stack and heap are parts of your computer's RAM, but they serve different purposes and follow different management rules.

The stack is a sequence of memory blocks, working in a LIFO—Last in, First out—manner. Whenever a function declares a variable, it is "pushed" onto the stack. And when the function exits, all its variables are "popped" off. The primary advantage of the stack is speed – it is incredibly fast to allocate and deallocate data from the stack.

The heap is where data with a longer lifecycle resides. When you dynamically allocate memory, it comes from the heap. Based on your program's design, this memory might exist for a short or long time period. Unlike stack, cleaning memory from the heap requires explicit commands – forget this, and you've got a classic memory leak.

3.5. Memory Safety: Avoiding Common Pitfalls

Memory safety involves preventing bugs and vulnerabilities associated with memory usage, like null or dangling pointers, buffer overflows, and unexpected alterations to data. Most languages equipped with manual memory management, like C and C++, are susceptible to these issues. Conversely, automatic memory management languages reduce the probability of these bugs but often at the cost of efficiency and control.

A key challenge in memory management is thus achieving robust memory safety without sacrificing speed and performance. This duality forms the backbone of Rust's novel memory management approach.

3.6. Rust: A Memory Management Revolution

As a programming language, Rust is unique in its commitment to providing power and performance without compromising safety. Its core principles surrounding memory safety and management challenge conventional methods.

Rust's memory management doesn't fit neatly into manual or automatic categories—it merges the best of both worlds, empowering developers with control over the system's memory as in manual memory management, while mitigating the related bugs and vulnerabilities. The upcoming sections will delve into these principles exhaustively.

No matter what other languages you've worked with, Rust's take on memory management is bound to present something new. Let's get ready to unlock the secret to concurrent computing without data races!

Chapter 4. Rust's Ownership Philosophy

At the heart of Rust's approach to safe and systematic memory management is a precise but straightforward philosophy: ownership. This seemingly simple concept offers profound practicalities, distinguishing Rust from many programming languages and positioning it uniquely within the persistent pursuit of efficient resource management.

4.1. The Core Tenets of Ownership

Rust's ownership system revolves around three primary rules:

1. Each value in Rust has a variable that is called its owner.

2. There can only be one owner at a time.

3. When the owner goes out of scope, the value will be dropped.

These rules form a distinctive, free-of-garbage-collector memory management system. Here, the compiler is equipped with enough information to ascertain when memory should be cleaned up, circumventing manual efforts prevalent in languages like C or C++.

4.2. Scope and Ownership

In determining ownership, Rust relies heavily on scope. Every time a variable is introduced in code, it comes with an associated block—or scope—where it is valid. For instance, consider the following:

```
{
    let s = "Hello, Rust!";
    println!("{}", s);
```

```
} // s goes out of scope and is dropped here
```

In this example, s becomes inaccessible beyond its scope.

4.3. Ownership Transfer: The "Move"

There are certain circumstances, however, where ownership of a value is transferred. Rust terms this as a "move". In this scenario, the original variable is rendered invalid. For instance:

```
let x = 5;
let y = x; // x is moved into y
println!("{}", x); // This will result in a compilation
error
```

Here, x gets moved into y, thereby x no longer becomes usable.

Alternatively, if you would simply like to duplicate data without altering ownership, cloning comes in handy. However, do be cognizant of the potential performance implications since this effectively creates a new heap allocation.

4.4. Borrowing with References

While ownership transfer is handy, Rust provides another option that allows value access without altering the ownership status quo: borrowing. To borrow a value, you can create a reference with the & symbol:

```
let s = String::from("Hello, Rust!");
let len = calculate_length(&s);
```

```
println!("The length of '{}' is {}.", s, len);

fn calculate_length(s: &String) -> usize {
    s.len()
}
```

In this example, `calculate_length` borrows s as a reference, permitting usage without taking ownership. In contrast to ownership, references in Rust allow shared read access. However, only one mutable reference is permissible within a scope to prevent data races in a concurrent scenario.

4.5. Rust's Borrow Checker

Rust's compiler also houses a robust analysis tool known as the "borrow checker". It provides a safety layer, verifying adherence to the borrowing rules at compile-time—guaranteeing safe concurrency by essentially eliminating data races.

4.6. Slice type: Another Form of Borrowing

Rust introduces another borrow form called a "slice"—a reference to a contiguous sequence within collection rather than the whole collection. It offers more flexibility without sacrificing ownership, thereby enhancing safety:

```
let s = String::from("Hello, Rust!");
let hello = &s[0..5];
let rust = &s[7..11];
```

This section of Rust's ownership philosophy only scratches the surface. As you delve and practice more, you will come to appreciate this unique system and how it synergizes with other features to construct a concurrent, fast, and safe programming model. For further exploration, consider Rust's official documentation and language book. Remember, while the journey may be challenging, the realization of safe concurrency without data races is well worth it.

Chapter 5. Conceptualizing Concurrency in Computing

Every complex problem, once dissected, becomes a mosaic of simpler, more manageable sub-problems. And so begins our journey into understanding concurrency, by breaking it down into smaller, digestible chunks to gradually demystify its intricacies.

On a fundamental level, concurrency is the occurrence of several tasks during overlapping time intervals. It is an organisational concept more than a temporal one - it's about managing more than one task independently and making progress on them simultaneously.

In computing, concurrency arises when various tasks can be started, run, and completed in overlapping time periods, rather than sequentially. It doesn't necessarily mean tasks will be executed at the same moment; rather, they might be intermittent, creating an illusion of parallelism.

5.1. Concurrency vs Parallelism

Before we delve further into concurrency, it's crucial to distinguish it from the seemingly similar yet decidedly different concept: parallelism.

While both concurrency and parallelism deal with 'doing more than one thing at a time', they have profoundly different characteristics and uses. Parallelism is about making tasks run faster, sometimes by simultaneously running them on different cores or processors. In contrast, concurrency is about managing lots of tasks at once.

In parallelism, multiple tasks are executed at the same time for faster completion, akin to running a race where the participant who finishes first wins. On the other hand, concurrency sets the stage for multiple tasks and allows them to make progress irrespective of the order in which they are completed.

5.2. Understanding Threads

At the heart of this discussion lies another important concept: the thread. A thread is the smallest sequence of programmed instructions that can be managed independently by a scheduler—part of the operating system's job. When we talk about concurrent execution, it is often the threads that we refer to.

There are two kinds of threads: OS threads and green threads. OS threads are managed by the operating system. They are truly concurrent, and can run on different processors. Green threads, on the other hand, are scheduled by the runtime of a language. They are usually more efficient, as they bypass some scheduler layers, but they may not benefit from multiple processors because they run in the same process.

5.3. The Task of Multithreading

Multithreading is a widespread technique to achieve concurrency in which multiple threads are created within a single process, sharing the process resources but able to execute independently.

Threads within a process can communicate with each other, as they share some resources, making task coordination possible. However, this shared state leads to one of the key aspects we need to consider when working on concurrency: race conditions.

5.4. Race Conditions: The Uninvited Guest

A `race condition` occurs when the program's behaviour is dependent on the relative order of execution of threads. This can lead to bugs or system vulnerabilities when threads manipulate shared data simultaneously.

When dealing with multiple threads, you, as a programmer, have nothing to ascertain the order in which different threads will execute. This lack of control can lead to situations where data is not processed reliably—leading to inconsistent outcomes and obscure bugs, every programmer's nightmare.

5.5. Memory Management in Concurrency

Shared memory situations expose another critical concept in concurrent computing: `memory management`.

Memory safety guarantees that a program will stop before it accesses a certain portion of memory. Memory safety bugs can manifest as elusive, pernicious issues, disrupting system integrity and security. Languages like C++, while giving programmers a high degree of control, also delegate memory management, leading to common bugs like null pointer deferencing and memory leaks.

Now consider a concurrent situation. The problems multiply manifold due to shared state and indeterminate thread execution order. Can we afford such unreliability in modern computing systems, where safety and efficiency must walk hand in hand?

This is where Rust's memory management paradigm comes into play, promising safer concurrency by tackling these issues head-on.

5.6. Rust: A Promise of Safe Concurrency

Rust is a system programming language that guarantees memory safety without needing a garbage collector. Through its core concepts of ownership with borrowing rules and lifetime tracking, Rust provides a powerful toolset to manage and control memory.

In the concurrency context, Rust's design eliminates common bugs due to race conditions, which are hard to debug and can lead to unexpected behaviors. By leveraging the ownership and type systems, Rust empowers programmers to resolve potential concurrency-related issues at compile-time.

While this brief overview serves as an introduction to the world of concurrency in computing, it's just the tip of the iceberg. Subsequent sections will delve deeper into various elements, and more importantly, how Rust navigates these turbulent waters safely. We will dissect the meaty topics of thread safety, handling shared state, and explore Rust's synchronous and asynchronous concurrency models.

From understanding the nuances introduced by shared mutable state to learning how to implement lock-free data structures, the adventurous journey of concurrency in Rust awaits. With every step along the way, we'll see how Rust brings an innovative and robust approach to achieve concurrency without falling into the traps of race conditions and memory management issues.

Chapter 6. Concurrency Concepts and Challenges in Traditional Languages

Concurrency is a critical element of modern programming, driven by the need for programs to handle multiple tasks seemingly in parallel. But before diving deep into the Rust factor, it is necessary to understand the basics, benefits, and pitfalls that concurrency offers in traditional languages.

6.1. What is Concurrency?

In programming, concurrency is the execution of the independent tasks in overlapping time phases. It differs from parallelism, where tasks literally run at the same time. Concurrency provides an illusion of parallelism by rapidly switching between tasks. Whether or not tasks indeed happen simultaneously depends on system architecture, specifically the number of cores on the CPU.

Concurrency aims to use system resources more efficiently, increase throughput, and improve responsiveness in interactive systems. Think of a web server handling hundreds of requests simultaneously yet individually, a typical example of concurrent execution.

6.2. Concurrency Models in Traditional Languages

Different programming languages implement concurrency differently. In broad strokes, there are shared state and message passing models:

1. Shared State Concurrency: Threads can read and write shared

data. In languages like Java, C++, programmers must meticulously manage access using mechanisms like locks, semaphores, and condition variables to avoid conflicts.

2. Message Passing Concurrency: This model decouples threads by disallowing shared state. Instead, threads communicate and synchronize by sending and receiving messages. Languages such as Erlang exemplify this model where shared state is indirectly achieved by passing messages containing data.

6.3. Challenges of Concurrency in Traditional Languages

Despite its compelling advantages, concurrency introduces a host of challenges often overlooked in sequential programming.

6.3.1. Data Races

A significant peril in concurrent programming is data races, occurring when two threads access the same memory location simultaneously, and at least one access is a write. Outcomes are non-deterministic making data races hard to debug.

6.3.2. Mutual Exclusion

Mutual exclusion involves ensuring that only one thread can access a shared resource at a given time. The challenge lies in implementing it correctly to prevent data inconsistency.

6.3.3. Deadlocks

Deadlock is a state where each thread is waiting for another to release a resource. None make progress, bringing the system to a standstill. The challenge is in designing your system in a way to avoid such deadlocks.

6.3.4. Starvation

Starvation happens when a thread is continually denied access to resources and can't make progress. It closely ties to the scheduling policies and can lead to sub-optimal usage of system resources.

6.4. Critical Section and Synchronization

In shared-state concurrency, the critical section refers to the part of the code where a thread accesses shared variables. Multiple threads must not execute the critical section simultaneously. Hence, synchronization primitives like locks, semaphores, and monitors are employed to protect the critical section.

However, using these primitives accurately and efficiently is notoriously complex, often leading to problems like deadlocks and starvation.

6.5. Context Switch Overhead

In multitasking environments, the system frequently switches from one task to another, called context switching. While necessary for concurrent execution, context switches introduce overhead, as the system must save and retrieve the task's state.

6.6. Performance

Concurrency does not always equate to faster execution. Due to overheads such as context switching, synchronization, and handling inter-thread communication, concurrent programs could potentially turn out slower than their sequential counterparts.

6.7. Threads vs Processes

Finally, while threads and processes are fundamental to operating system design and getting concurrency right in programming languages, it's also fertile ground for confusion. Threads share the same virtual memory, making communication more straightforward. However, this also increases the likelihood of data races. Processes have isolated memory, reducing data race probability but complicating communication between processes.

This brief look into concurrency's concepts and challenges underscores the complexity and the need for safer, concurrent language constructs. Enter Rust, a language that infuses these lessons in its very design to ensure safe concurrency free of data races. It adheres to the 'don't act surprised' notion by refusing to compile code that's ambivalent in its safety, particularly concerning concurrency. In the subsequent section, we will unravel how Rust achieves this without compromising execution efficiency.

Chapter 7. Rust's Unique Approach to Concurrency

Rust's defining feature is its unique take on handling concurrent programming, a highly desirable yet complex feature that is fraught with pitfalls. The language manages to provide a level of safety and elegance in a domain where traditionally, increased functionality means proportionally increased chances of encountering dangerous bugs. This is achieved by two key principles: ownership and borrowing.

7.1. Ownership and Borrowing

The ownership system in Rust has three main rules:

1. Each value in Rust is assigned to a variable, which is known as the owner.
2. There can be only one owner at a time.
3. When the owner goes out of scope, the value is dropped.

Borrowing, on the other hand, allows for data to be used without taking ownership of it. Rust has two types of borrowing: mutable and immutable.

7.2. Concurrent Programming in Rust

Rust applies these principles to concurrent programming, making it safer and more ergonomic than in other languages. Traditionally, when threads share data, they can easily get into the state of data races. But Rust applies strict constraints to avoid these situations while also making parallel programming more efficient.

7.3. The Problem of Shared Mutable State

The possibility of data races arises when three conditions are met:

1. Two or more pointers access the same data at the same time.

2. At least one of the pointers modifies the data.

3. There's no mechanism being used to synchronize access to the data.

If we can prevent even one of these conditions from being true, the program will be free of data races. Rust achieves this by restricting the scenarios where three conditions might occur. Rust opts for compile-time check rather than a runtime check to prevent these races.

7.4. Threads in Rust

Rust has native support for threads, allowing concurrent execution of parts of a program. Thread creation is handled by the std::thread library, and communications between threads are handled by the std::sync library.

When a new thread is created using the `thread::spawn` function, Rust ensures safety by using its ownership system. The spawned closure must encompass `'static` lifetime, meaning it must not borrow values (excluding those with `'static` lifetime), including its parameters.

Here's a simple example of thread creation:

```
use std::thread;

fn main() {
    thread::spawn(|| {
```

```
        // this code will be executed in a new thread
        println!("Hello from a thread!");
    });
}
```

Rust maintains safety by enforcing rules about which variables are accessible from the new thread and which ones are not, using its borrowing and ownership systems.

7.5. Message Passing Concurrency in Rust

Unlike other languages where shared memory concurrency is a norm, Rust leans towards a message-passing model. This model operates by having threads communicate by sending each other messages containing data. A major advantage of message-passing concurrency is that there's no way for a thread to accidentally corrupt the data of another, as is possible with shared-memory concurrency.

Here's an example of using channels, a Rust construct for message-passing concurrency:

```
use std::sync::mpsc;
use std::thread;

fn main() {
    let (tx, rx) = mpsc::channel();

    thread::spawn(move || {
        tx.send("Hello from a thread!").unwrap();
    });

    println!("Message: {}", rx.recv().unwrap());
```

```
}
```

This program creates a channel with `mpsc::channel`. `mpsc` stands for multiple producer, single consumer. With this type of channel, multiple sending ends can send messages to one receiving end.

7.6. Mutex in Rust

A Mutex - short for mutual exclusion, is a synchronisation primitive useful for protecting shared data. Rust's std::sync::Mutex struct represents a mutex.

By using the lock method on a Mutex, you acquire the lock and get a MutexGuard representing that lock. A MutexGuard is a smart pointer, and while you hold it, you have exclusive access to the data.

Here's a brief example:

```
use std::sync::Mutex;

let m = Mutex::new(5);

{
    let mut num = m.lock().unwrap();
    *num = 6;
}

println!("m = {:?}", m);
```

The mutex is a complex structure compared to channels, however, it is efficient and good for certain performance-critical sections.

Rust's embrace of ownership, borrowing, thread safety, message-passing concurrency, and mutexes, all work together to manage the complexity of concurrent programming. These tools not only prevent data-race conditions but also bring about highly efficient, performant, and safer programs.

This unique approach ensures developers can write multi-threaded code with confidence, knowing the pitfalls often associated with such tasks are tactfully avoided. Rust ensures that concurrent programming doesn't have to be a trade-off between safety and performance, making it an increasingly popular choice for systems programming.

Chapter 8. Safeguarding Memory Access in Threads

To deeply understand Rust's guardian approach to memory access within threads, we will unfold its workings through three vital components – Ownership, Borrowing, and Lifetimes. Comprehending these concepts is pivotal to unraveling concurrency in Rust that ensures memory safety.

8.1. Understanding Ownership

In Rust, each value has a specific variable tagged as its owner. There can only be one owner at any given moment, and when the owner goes out of scope, the value will be dropped.

Rust uses the concept of ownership to manage memory via a system of compile-time checks, with no extra runtime cost. This effectively prevents runtime bugs related to memory, such as null pointer dereferencing, double free, and dangling pointers, among others.

Consider the following example:

```
fn main() {
    let s = String::from("hello"); // s is the owner
} // s goes out of scope, "hello" is dropped
```

Here, s owns the String "hello". When s goes out of scope at the end of the main function, the memory allocated for "hello" gets automatically deallocated.

8.2. The Concept of Borrowing

Often, we might need to access a data location without taking ownership of it. Here is where Borrowing steps in. In Rust, we can borrow references to a value, rather than taking its ownership.

There are two types of Borrowing - Mutable and Immutable. An essential trait of Rust is that these references abide by a set of rules enforced at compile time:

- There can be an unlimited number of immutable references.

- There can only be one mutable reference and no immutable ones.

This crucial rule ensures Rust's major goals of memory safety and concurrency without data races, since it strictly prevents simultaneous access for both reading and writing.

A simple illustration of borrowing is as follows:

```
fn main() {
    let mut s = String::from("hello");
    let s1 = &mut s; // mutable borrow
    let s2 = &s; // immutable borrow is not allowed,
compilation fails
    let s3 = &s; // immutable borrow is not allowed,
compilation fails
    println!("{}, {}", s1, s2);
}
```

In this example, the code fails to compile because while there is a mutable reference to s (i.e., &mut s or s1), the program attempts to create immutable references (s2 and s3). Rust's safety checks at compile time come into play here, preventing potential data races.

8.3. Lifetimes and their Role

The last piece of the puzzle in safe memory management lies with Lifetimes. They define the period for which a reference remains valid.

Although lifetimes are implicit and inferred most of the time, there are scenarios in Rust where they must be explicitly annotated to avoid potential 'dangling reference' problems. An explicit lifetime looks like this:

```
fn longest<'a>(x: &'a str, y: &'a str) -> &'a str {
    if x.len() > y.len() {
        x
    } else {
        y
    }
}
```

In this function, 'a is the lifetime annotation that implies that both string slices x and y, along with the return type, have the same lifetime. This guarantees Rust's memory safety by ensuring the returned reference will not outlive either of the input references.

8.4. Working with Shared State in Concurrency

In concurrent situations, we often find multiple threads need access to shared data. Rust's standard library offers primitive types for concurrent, mutable shared state operations in the form of Mutex<T> and RwLock<T>.

In Rust, a Mutex<T> represents a mutual exclusion primitive useful for protecting shared data. Any thread can lock the Mutex<T> and then access the data it guards. Once the thread is done, other threads can then lock it.

```rust
use std::sync::Mutex;

fn main() {
    let data = Mutex::new(5);

    {
        let mut num = data.lock().unwrap();
        *num = 6;
    }

    println!("data = {:?}", data);
}
```

The data is locked, mutated, and then unlocked on scope exit, keeping the operation safe from data races. Rust additionally ensures that the Mutex will always be unlocked properly, even if a panic occurs while the lock is held.

Understanding the intricacies of memory management in Rust such as Ownership, Borrowing, Lifetimes, and managing shared states can lead to a programming approach that anticipates and prevents problems ahead of time. With Rust, developers can look forward to handling threading with no fear of common memory safety issues or data races. This is the heart of Rust's safe and efficient concurrency.

Chapter 9. The Role of Fearless Concurrency

Modern computing often involves running several processes in parallel, primarily to exploit the efficiency inherent in any chip with multiple cores. Indeed, multi-threaded programming has become one of the central elements of modern computer architecture. However, this efficiency boon comes with a significant challenge: to manage concurrency in a manner that prevents data corruption. Enter "fearless concurrency," an idea that forms the core of the Rust language's approach to memory management.

9.1. Understanding Data Races

Before delving into the Rust's concurrency tactics, it's critical to comprehend what exactly it counteracts: the phenomenon of data races. Data races occur when two or more threads concurrently access the same location in memory, and at least one of these accesses is a write operation. When these conditions conspire without any measure of synchronization in place, chaos ensues. The outcome? A system full of unpredictability. Your code begins to behave peculiarly and data integrity swoons into jeopardy.

Any web server or operating system thrives on handling several tasks in parallel. Emails stream in, file uploads get processed, databases perform transactions, users log in and out—all simultaneously. Traditional programming languages, in attempting to manage concurrency, often leave sufficient headroom for data races to manifest, inviting various challenges to reliability and performance.

9.2. The Fearless Concurrency Principle

We witness the emergence of "fearless concurrency". Rust empowers programmers to construct their applications in a way where such catastrophes are potentially impossible by design. The principle drives memory safety sans garbage collection and shields programs from synchronization errors, thus making concurrent programming fear-less.

For instance, Rust's unique take on how to manage memory, combined with its strict compiler, safeguards developers from concurrency-related danger zones. The language's ownership model ensures that a given piece of memory can't be accessed by two different threads simultaneously unless there are explicit safeguards. As a result, Rust allows coding complex, multi-threaded applications with significantly reduced scope for data races.

9.3. Deconstructing Memory Management in Rust

The heuristic imperative to Rust's reliable memory management lies in its ownership schema. It has a set of rules checked at compile time that don't require a garbage collector running in the background to clean up unused memory.

Rust relies on three principles for its memory model:

- Ownership: A piece of memory can have only one owner, and this owner is responsible for destroying the memory when it is no longer needed.

- Borrowing: While a value is borrowed, the owner cannot manipulate it.

- Lifetime: This refers to the scape where a particular reference is valid.

Although Rust introduces some constraints, it does so with the noble intent of keeping developers and their applications safe. By advocating strong, static typing and an emphasis on compile-time error checking, it drives developers to handle potential errors before they snowball into a bleak mess.

9.4. The Magic of Ownership, Borrowing, and Lifetime

The ownership model's central tenet, expressed simply, is that a given value can have exactly one owner: a variable. If this variable goes out of scope, then the value is automatically "dropped", freeing any associated resources. What enables Rust to achieve this is the concept of "ownership" with the so-called RAII (Resource Acquisition Is Initialization) paradigm, where every object has one—and only one—responsible owner.

This is coupled closely with the concepts of "borrowing" and "lifetime". A reference in Rust can either be mutable where it can be used to modify the associated data, or it can be immutable, where the data cannot be modified using this reference.

An essential variant of borrowing is "mutable borrowing". This happens when you want to allow a piece of code to modify your value. Rust enforces that while this mutable borrow is alive, you can't make any other borrows. This gives Rust the power to prevent data races at compile time.

The "lifetime" concept in Rust refers to the scope in which references can be used. If references were allowed to be used regardless of the lifetime of the source, it would be next to impossible to ensure memory safety. Rust's system of lifetimes helps it prevent this kind of scenario.

9.5. Final Thoughts on Fearless Concurrency

It's not that Rust has invented a way to make concurrency trivial. Instead, what Rust has done is avoid some common pitfalls associated with concurrent programming by making these errors impossible at the compiler level. Encapsulated in the maxim "fearless concurrency", Rust's unique approach to memory management marks a novel way to write efficient and safe multi-threaded code.

In conclusion, Rust's rising popularity comes as no surprise when considering its powerful memory safety features and "fearless concurrency". Much like how our society has safety rules to prevent accidents, Rust's strict laws regarding memory management serve to keep data races at bay. Thus, Rust holds a promising future in the realm of systems programming, and potentially, anywhere else high performance is a must.

Chapter 10. Case Studies: Avoiding Data Races in Rust

Data races have been an unsolved problem in concurrent computing since its inception. Rust's approach to solving this problem takes a pattern of 'ownership and borrowing', and 'lifetimes' in conjunction with the fearless concurrency. Here, we'll dissect multiple real-world scenarios where Rust's model prevents data races.

10.1. A Simple Mutex

Consider this simple case involving a mutex (mutual exclusion), a common tool for preventing multiple threads from accessing a shared resource simultaneously. The intuitive way of using a mutex is by 'locking' it before accessing the shared resource, and 'unlocking' it after completing.

```rust
use std::sync::Mutex;
use std::thread;

fn main() {
    let m = Mutex::new(5);

    {
        let mut num = m.lock().unwrap();
        *num = 6;
    }

    println!("m = {:?}", m);
}
```

In the above code, we create a `Mutex<T>` object named `m`. The `lock` method, as the name suggests, locks access to the shared resource and returns a mutable reference that can be dereferenced. Post access, the dropped `MutexGuard` automatically unlocks the mutex owing to Rust's RAII (Resource Acquisition Is Initialization) guarantee.

Under the Rust paradigm, the mutex ensures that the thread accessing the shared data has exclusive access rights, thereby ruling out the possibility of a data race.

10.2. Spreadsheet: Safe Multithreaded Calculations

Consider implementing a simple spreadsheet with the capability to dynamically update the dependent cells - a classic case of shared mutable state. How can Rust handle this without data races?

The core idea is to structure the dependencies in an Acyclic Graph. Each node in the graph is protected by a Mutex. When a cell's value changes, its dependent cells are updated. Here's a simplified version of the implementation:

```rust
use std::sync::{Arc, Mutex};

// A 'Cell' represents a cell in the spreadsheet.
pub struct Cell {
    value: f64,
    dependent_cells: Vec<Arc<Mutex<Cell>>>,
}

impl Cell {
    // Changing the value of the cell.
    pub fn change_value(&mut self, new_val: f64) {
        self.value = new_val;
        self.update_dependents();
    }
```

```
        // Updating the value in the dependent cells.
        fn update_dependents(&self) {
            for cell in &self.dependent_cells {
                let mut locked_cell = cell.lock().unwrap();
                locked_cell.change_value(self.value * 2.0);
// Sample formula
            }
        }
}
```

Here, the `Mutex` around each `Cell` distributes the ownership among threads safely and ensures no thread updates a 'Cell' while it's being updated by another. With this, implementing a dynamic and concurrent Spreadsheet is achievable in Rust without data races!

10.3. Banking System: Safe Transactions

Consider the setting of a banking system that handles transactions simultaneously. Traditional languages often struggle to handle complex, multithreaded transaction processing without data races. Let's explore how Rust tackles this problem:

```
use std::sync::{Arc, Mutex};
use std::thread;

pub struct Account {
    balance: Mutex<i32>,
}

impl Account {
    // Creates new account with a provided balance
    pub fn new(amount: i32) -> Account {
```

```
        Account { balance: Mutex::new(amount) }
    }

    // Transfers amount from self to target account
    pub fn transfer(&self, target: &Account, amount:
i32) {
        let mut self_balance =
self.balance.lock().unwrap();
        let mut target_balance =
target.balance.lock().unwrap();

        if *self_balance >= amount {
            *self_balance -= amount;
            *target_balance += amount;
        }
    }
}

fn main() {
    let john = Arc::new(Account::new(100));
    let paul = Arc::new(Account::new(50));

    let transfer = thread::spawn({
        let john_clone = Arc::clone(&john);
        let paul_clone = Arc::clone(&paul);

        move || {
            john_clone.transfer(&paul_clone, 30);
        }
    });

    transfer.join().unwrap();

    assert_eq!(*john.balance.lock().unwrap(), 70);
    assert_eq!(*paul.balance.lock().unwrap(), 80);
```

```
    }
```

In Rust, each account's balance is owned by a Mutex and synchronized. Transferring between accounts will lock each involved account first, preventing any accesses from other threads while the operation is in progress.

These case studies demonstrate Rust's effectiveness as a guardian against data races in concurrent computations. Whether it's a simple mutex or complex operations in a banking system, Rust ensures thread safety without compromising on the performance and efficiency of applications.

Chapter 11. Future Perspectives: Rust and Concurrency

In the modern landscape of computing, concurrently executed threads have carved their way to a position of paramount significance. The manifestation of concurrent computing in applications pertaining to databases, server handling, and data processing is both pervasive and instrumental. Yet, it is equally notorious to be a breeding ground for conundrums, chiefly, the dreaded data races. Crucially, the language Rust equips developers with a paradigm that assuredly mitigates these data race cases, paving the way for safe, lightning-paced performance of concurrent systems in the foreseeable future.

Concurrent computing in Rust does more than merely keeping pace with the demands of modern software systems - it revolutionizes the entire paradigm with a refreshing and safer alternative. Leveraging Rust's strong type system and guarantees around memory safety, developers can leverage the speed of multi-core processors without the traditional pitfalls of multithreaded programming.

11.1. Rust's Memory Safety Safeguards

Rust's memory safety model is an integral facet of its approach to concurrency. With its ownership system and the safety measures provided by the borrow checker, it erects robust partitions against data races. Structurally, every data entity in Rust has a precise 'owner', and that ownership can be transferred, avoiding significant issues related to data races and memory usage.

In the context of concurrency, the ownership system plays a considerable role. When multiple threads need to access or modify a shared value, Rust's safety guards ensure that only one thread can actively modify the data at a given time. The other threads can only read the data when it is ensured that no modifications are in progress. This dramatically simplifies the process of concurrent memory management, significantly reducing the complexity developers have to grapple with.

11.2. Rust's Fearless Concurrency

Threading in Rust takes a different approach compared to other languages. The threads in Rust can be seen as independent units within the program, each with its own stack and local state. But Rust doesn't leave you with just the raw threads - it provides several higher-level concurrency abstractions, such as `Arc`, `Mutex`, `RwLock`, and `channel`, that encapsulate multi-threaded programming constructs behind a safer, more accessible interface.

The 'fearless concurrency' Rust offers consolidates the utilization of these higher-level constructs, ensuring that threads interact without engendering common multithreading issues. These constructs maximize the safety and predictability in systems that require high efficiency in managing concurrent operations. Expect these features to greatly influence programming languages of the future, setting higher benchmarks for safety and concurrency performance.

11.3. Channels - A Paradigm Shift

Rust also introduces a channel system for thread communication, a paradigm that deviates from the conventional 'shared data' approach employed by most languages. Instead of threads contending for data ownership, Rust channels facilitate communication via message passing. Threads can send (or receive) values of a certain type, effectively enabling concurrent, inter-thread conversations.

The sending is performed via the Sender, and the messages received are read from the Receiver - a concept famously known as 'senders and receivers'. These two halves communicate via a shared channel. The channel's transmitter will be cloned for each thread that requires to send a message. This model eliminates the potential of race conditions, as the threads no longer need to use shared, mutable data. Channels in Rust is a promising concept that we might see further evolution of in the future.

11.4. The Potential Impact of Rust's Concurrency Model

Rust's concurrency model is claimed to be a game-changer in modern computing. It provides clear-cut safety guarantees that eliminate data races, encouraging developers to write more concurrent programs. This could lead to a significant improvement in the performance of software systems, as multi-threaded programming becomes safer and more accessible.

In the future, the programming landscape might witness an increased adoption of Rust-like memory safety features and higher-level concurrency abstractions. More languages could start to primarily focus on specifying clear ownership and borrowing rules for memory safety, rather than leaving it up to developers. We are looking at an emergence of programming languages that are not only safe by default but can exploit the full potential of hardware architectures.

In conclusion, Rust sets the groundwork for a future where concurrency is not a barrier but instead, a tool for developers to write faster and more efficient software. Its unique handling of memory safety and concurrency, through ownership rules and high-level abstractions, could be seen as a beacon lighting the way towards a safer and more efficient multi-threaded programming world.

11.5. Rust's Growing Appeal and Future Research Directions

However revolutionary, Rust's concurrent computing strategy is still in its adolescence, continually maturing with advancements introduced by an enthusiastic community of developers and researchers.

As for future directions, an invigorating opportunity for research lies around making concurrency even more accessible for developers. An important part of this would be in minimizing the learning curve for new users while expanding the set of concurrency primitives offered in the standard library.

A future conception of Rust may also see more sophisticated type systems bolstering existing constructs, possibly introducing runtime systems that further enhance safety and efficiency. We may see a surge of interest in developing tools to facilitate the analysis, testing, and verification of Rust concurrent programs.

Finally, Rust's application in major industries, particularly in system programming and in web assembly, is only expected to increase. With such unstoppable momentum, it is conceivable that Rust's concurrency capabilities might become the gold standard for other programming languages in the not-so-distant future. Indeed, the future shines bright for Rust and concurrency.